Handbags

A Collector's Guide

Tracy Tolkien

MILLER'S HANDBAGS: A COLLECTOR'S GUIDE
by Tracy Tolkien

First published in Great Britain in 2001 by Miller's, a division of Mitchell Beazley, imprints of Octopus Publishing Group Ltd, 2–4 Heron Quays, London E14 4JP

Miller's is a registered trademark of Octopus Publishing Group Ltd

Commissioning Editor **Anna Sanderson**
Executive Art Editor **Rhonda Fisher**
Project Editor **Emily Anderson**
Designer **Louise Griffiths**
Editor **Anthea Snow**
Indexer **Sue Farr**
Picture Research **Maria Gibbs, Nick Wheldon**
Production **Nancy Roberts**
Jacket photography by **Steve Tanner**

ISBN 1 84000 430 4

A CIP catalogue record for this book is available from the British Library
Set in Bembo, Frutiger and Shannon
Produced by Toppan Printing Co., (HK) Ltd.
Printed and bound in China

Jacket illustrations, front cover, clockwise from top: Black leather, calf and crocodile bag, 1950s, American, unsigned, **£60–90/$90–135**; crystal and gilt beaded bag, 1960s, American, unsigned, **£40–60/$60–90**; cloth and sequin bag, 1930s, American, unsigned, **£60–90/$90–135**; gilt metal *minaudière*, 1950s, American, signed "Evans", **£120–140/$180–210** Back cover: Beaded bag with celluloid frame, 1920s, French, signed "Made in France", **£180–220/$270–330** Half-title page: Hand-painted satin clutch, 1920s, French, unsigned, **£70–90/$105–135**; Contents page: Bead and embroidered cloth bag in "Arts & Crafts" style, English, unsigned, **£220–250/$330–375**

contents

Introduction

After decades of charity-shop (thrift-shop) obscurity, vintage fashion has become one of the hottest new categories in collecting today. Clothing, costume jewellery and handbags are now increasingly sought after and prices are rising fast. Handbags are particularly popular because they are fun and easy to mix with today's vintage-inspired clothing styles. While collectable handbags come in all shapes and sizes, you will not find many of the ordinary, serviceable bags that most of us carry today. Instead, it is the special, surprising or exquisite handbags that collectors crave.

Early forms from the Middle Ages and beyond are well worth studying in museums, but the handbag as we know it emerged in the 19thC and therefore most personal collections begin at this point. The history of the handbag is inevitably related to the history of fashion, so look out for bags that strongly express the style of a particular era. It is also good to go for pieces that reflect important

Bead and gilt bag, 1940s, American, signed "Fre-Mor", **£180–220/$270–330**

decorative and artistic trends such as Arts and Crafts, Art Deco, Pop Art and psychedelia.

As with mainstream collecting, the condition of the piece is vital, so a pristine 1960s Pucci handbag might well be worth £650/$1,000, while the same bag if faded or torn would be lucky to fetch a tenth of that price. Collectors prefer unused bags. Special evening styles were carefully looked after and seldom worn, and therefore examples from all eras can turn up in perfect condition.

Always check both the inside and the outside of a bag. Dealers often stuff bags with tissue paper, so make sure that you remove this before you buy: discouraging damage or encouraging designer signatures could be hidden underneath the paper.

Many marks or signatures add nothing to value, but certain key names, such as "Hermès" or "Cartier", could mean that you have struck vintage gold. Be sure that you also examine a handbag's frame on the inside and the outside, since marks here can be tiny and difficult to spot. Most bags, however, are unsigned, so you have to train your eye. Before you start your collection, visit shops, markets and antique centres. Do not be afraid to ask questions even

Embroidered cloth bag, late 19thC, English, unsigned, **£400–500/$600–750**

if you do not intend to buy. Most dealers are passionate about their subject and love to talk, realizing that an interested browser could easily become a good customer in the future.

Read all the reference books that you can find and visit your local library, where you can ask for back issues of fashion magazines, decade-by-decade. Most libraries keep such an archive. These magazines will give you a feel for the typical look of various eras and help you to identify and date your vintage finds.

There are many different approaches to collecting handbags. Some enthusiasts go for anything that appeals to them, while others confine themselves to a particular decade or era. Some like to collect by category, such as box bags or baskets, or to focus on specific materials, such as beads, mesh or bakelite.

Prices for good bags are certainly rising, but keep in mind that these are a fashion-orientated item so demand mirrors current trends. Tom Ford's revamp at Gucci at the start of the new millennium has led to a dramatic rise in prices for older Gucci bags. Once this trend cools, however, vintage prices will probably fall. Fashion will always be fickle, so by all means go for the best you can comfortably afford, but purchase only those pieces that you feel you must have. Vintage fashion will never be an area for purely speculative investment, but it does bring other rewards.

Consider the sheer romanticism of carrying a bag that was once treasured and important to an unknown woman of the distant past. She may have kept her crystal vial of smelling salts in the very pocket where you now tuck your flip-top mobile phone. And yet you have both experienced the same pleasure in dressing up and going out. Although fashion changes, the enjoyment of it stays the same. Collecting and wearing vintage handbags is a wonderful way of staying in touch with what it has always meant to be a fashionable woman.

It is lovely to carry a glittering, decorative confection that draws attention to its wearer and yet still somehow manages to keep her secrets. Fashion editors have long claimed that you can judge a woman by the quality of her handbag. But no one has ever claimed to be able to guess what she carries inside.

Faux-ivory bag with openwork dragons and silk lining, c.1920s, French, signed "Deposé J.M."
£280–380/$420–570

Early bags

While 15th and 16thC bags can be viewed in museums, and turn up in the salerooms of top auction houses, most mainstream collections begin with those from the 19thC. Handbags had always been made at home as part of domestic needlework duties, but their commercial manufacture really took off in the 1800s. Both types can be collectable, and many 19thC bags survive that are not prohibitively expensive today. Bags from that period are often loosely termed "Victorian", in reference to Queen Victoria's long reign (1837–1901). As with any textile items, early bags have often deteriorated, so check condition carefully and avoid using those made of fabric, as such bags are usually too fragile.

▼ Chatelaines
Chatelaine bags were not carried in the hand but instead dangled from a belt worn at the waist. They are easily identified by their characteristic hook fastening, usually found at the apex of a chain handle.

Ring-mesh chatelaine bag, c.1890, probably German, unsigned, **£150–200/ $225–300**

◄ Cut steel
Steel beads cut from long metal rods had been used to decorate clothing since the late 18thC, but were particularly popular in the Victorian period. Here cut-steel beads are embroidered on black velvet in a typically French, medieval-style, heraldic design. Cut-steel studs reminiscent of 19thC costume jewellery appear on the clasp. The superb detail and pristine condition make this bag a collector's dream.

Cut-steel and velvet bag, c.1880, probably French, unsigned, **£700–800/ $1,050– 1,200**

• Water is the natural
enemy of cut steel,
so make sure that such
bags are kept dry. Before
you buy check carefully
for rust, as this seriously
lowers value.
• "French jet" is black
glass made to imitate
the real thing. It appears
shinier and heavier than
genuine jet.

"Miser's purse", c.1860,
probably English, unsigned,
£50–75/$75–110

▲ The "miser's purse"

Both men and women used
the "miser's purse", or
"stocking bag", for carrying
change. Coins were slipped
into a central opening and
then secured at either end
with metal sliders. As with
chatelaines these were not
carried in the hand, but were
worn slung over a belt or kept
in a pocket or larger handbag.
Such purses were handknitted,
often by children, and given
as gifts to parents and friends.

▼ Pockets

The earliest handbags were, in
effect, detached pockets that
were tied around the waist
and worn underneath a
voluminous skirt. Like the
elaborate lace underclothing
that was never put on public
display, these early pockets
were often beautiful and
highly decorated. The Neo-
classical fashions of the late
18thC hugged the figure
closely, causing pockets to
bulge unattractively, so the
hand-held bag or reticule
quickly replaced this style.

Pastoral-print silk pocket, late
18thC, probably English, unsigned,
£150–200/$225–300

Jet and silk
drawstring bag,
c.1860s,
probably
English, unsigned,
£50–75/$75–110

▲ Mourning bags

Bags such as these were
carried by Victorians in full
mourning, since protocol
required them to dress
entirely in black. Jet beads
were used to decorate
mourning clothes as well as
jewellery and handbags. This
bag was probably made by
its original owner.

Beaded bags

Beads have long been embroidered onto cloth bags for decorative effect, but collectors particularly love the type that is made by knitting perhaps thousands of tiny beads into a continuous carpet that becomes the bag itself. Worked by candlelight, on needles as slender as wire, such bags could take many months to complete. While some were sold commercially at staggeringly high prices, many are highly personal home creations. A beaded bag might commemorate the loss of a loved one and display the traditional iconography of mourning, such as willows, urns or churchyard scenes. Other, more cheerful examples may be signed and dated, like needlework samplers. Beaded bags were popular from the early 19thC to the 1920s, and enjoyed a huge revival in the 1950s.

▼ **Figurals**
These are the most valuable of all beaded bags. They can depict landscapes, such as this river scene, or people, animals, ships, cottages, castles and famous cities. Mythical, pastoral and religious subjects were often copied from tapestries or popular prints and so reflect contemporary decorative trends. The most valuable figurals are complex, finely detailed designs.

Beaded figural bag with gilt clasp, c.1860, probably German, unsigned, **£500–700/$750–1,050**

Large, beaded drawstring bag (relined), c.1850s, possibly English, unsigned, **£175–275/ $260–410**

◀ **Florals**
Although technically figural, floral designs were so common that serious collectors do not take a strong interest in them unless a bag is unusually large, or the beading is remarkably fine. Check inside to see if the drawstring threads through original tortoiseshell or ivory rings; these were used for better-quality bags.

• Figurals in the style
of American folk art and
patterns reminiscent of
oriental rugs can both
be extremely valuable.
• The best steel beads
were made in France,
while Venice led the
market in glass beads.
• The most sought-after
bags use tiny beads,
sometimes as fine as
a grain of sand.

▼ **Colourful cut steel**
By the early 20thC,
cut-steel beads came
in a range of colours.
These bags are now
highly collectable,
but few survive because
the weight of the cut
steel tended to pull
the underlying threads
apart. The best examples
were made in France.

Cut-steel bag, c.1914, French,
signed "Made in France",
£200–300/$300–450

Beaded bag with gilt clasp,
c.1870s, probably English,
unsigned, **£200–300/$300–450**

▲ **Double-sided figurals**
This charming little figural has
a windmill on one side and a
songbird on the other. Value is
further enhanced by its pretty
gilt clasp and perfect fringing.
Check fringing carefully as it
is vulnerable to loss and
restoration is expensive.

▼ **Art Deco beading**
Bold, geometric beading and
an Egyptian-style clasp date
this bag to the 1920s. The
clasp is made of celluloid, a
form of plastic widely used to
imitate ivory. Such clasps were
often tinted or set with paste
stones. Celluloid is highly
collectable but fragile, so
check its condition carefully.

Beaded bag with celluloid clasp
and handle, 1920s, French, signed
"Deposé", **£400–500/
$600–750**

From Victorian to Edwardian

As the world became increasingly industrialized, commercially produced bags flooded the market. Companies vied for the consumer's attention with new types of frames, clasps and materials. Women took advantage of this boom and wore several chatelaines at once, or filled larger bags with a variety of smaller ones. For the first time there was a true variation in size: from huge crocodile travelling cases to tiny silver change purses. It is often difficult to place earlier bags precisely, but some mass-produced products were stamped with a date in connection with a patent number, or were engraved by their original owners. Bags are referred to as "Edwardian" if made during the reign of Edward VII (1901–1910), while later 20thC examples are usually classed by their decade.

▼ Metal frames
Intricate metal frames were popular in the late 19th and early 20thC, and these were often paired with simple leather or fabric bodies. Look out for Art Nouveau designs of sinuous flowers and plants, or female figures with long, flowing hair. This bag bears a silver hallmark on the outside of its frame.

Art Nouveau silver and cloth bag, c.1900, English, signed with hallmarks
£200–300/ $300–450

Engraved metal coin purse, c.1880s, English, signed "RFDC",
£65–85/ $95–125

▲ Metal bags
Metal finger-ring purses, such as this one, came in silver, gold or silver plate. This one is stamped "E.P.N.S.", which means that it is plated and therefore worth less than a solid-silver piece.

Art Nouveau leather bag, c.1900, probably English, unsigned, **£100–200/$150–300**

▲ **Leather bags**
Since leather bags were a favourite for everyday use, many that survive are now badly worn. The value of this chatelaine is enhanced by its good condition and fine, Art Nouveau, gilt-metal frame decorated with swirling irises.

▼ **Recycling frames**
The velvet body of this sporran-style bag is now badly damaged and probably beyond repair. However, an elaborate Victorian steel frame such as this one is well worth having and could easily be recycled with new fabric or, better still, an antique remnant. It would then become an interesting and highly wearable bargain.

Velvet and steel-chain bag, c.1890, English, unsigned, **£20–40/$30–60**

FACT FILE

• Many early frames are made of "German silver", an alloy of zinc, copper and nickel. Although it is more robust than true silver, it is not as valuable.
• Look out for sentimental Victorian coin purses bearing messages such as "Be Mine" or "Sweetheart". These are typical of the period and inexpensive.

Celluloid and calfskin pocket case, c.1910, English, unsigned, **£145–165/$215–245**

▲ **Pocket cases**
Although pocket cases had been used since the 18thC, by the 19th they had become increasingly complex, with interior compartments for letters, stamps, visiting cards and coins. Many also came with a small notebook and pencil inside. The decoration here is particularly detailed: faux-ivory knights are shown at a joust, complete with an audience picked out in embossed leather.

Home-made bag with needlepoint cottage scene, c.1910, English, unsigned, **£90–130/$135–195**

▲ **Needlepoint**
In the early 20thC most women led what would now be considered highly restrictive lives, which denied them higher education, jobs and even much freedom of movement. Without cinema, television or radio, needlework provided a welcome distraction and occupied time constructively. In fact, doctors recommended it as a cure for restless anxiety. Unlike commercially produced needlepoint (see p.28), this charming bag was probably made by its original owner.

▼ **Home creations**
Ladies could turn their domestic needlework into a finished bag by stitching it to a frame, which was sold separately. More ambitious home creations were mounted professionally. Unlike early fabric, lace or beaded bags, needlepoint bags are often strong enough to withstand occasional, careful use.

Home-made needlepoint bag with herons on a steel frame, c.1890, English, unsigned, **£120–160/ $180–240**

Crocheted silk sewing bag, c.1910, American, unsigned, **£40–60/$60–90**

▲ **Crochet**
Petit point, needlepoint and beading were usually reserved for special home-made bags, while crochet was used on more ordinary and functional ones. This drawstring bag was made to hold sewing implements and needlework in progress. With all fabric, but especially in the case of needlework bags, fading or soiling lowers value considerably. Dry cleaning is rarely successful with early textiles.

Linings
Early linings were often silk, which is especially vulnerable to shattering. The absence of a lining does not, therefore, necessarily detract from a fine antique bag. A good-quality replacement lining in the original style can even add value.

FACT FILE

Leather and gilt wallet, c.1890, Irish, unsigned, **£20–40/$30–60**

▲ **Decorated leather**
Early purses and bags are always more collectable when they reflect contemporary decorative trends. Look out for leathers embossed with Arts and Crafts or Art Nouveau designs. These can be valuable if condition is good. Silver or gilt decorations overlaid on leather can also be valuable, but this wallet is in poor condition and the design is not good enough to command a top price.

▼ **Shattering**
This gold-lace bag is attractive but unfortunately it has started to "shatter". The fabric is in an irreversible state of decay and will disintegrate even with gentle handling. This often happens with antique textiles that have been improperly stored.

Lace and bead drawstring bag, c.1850, English, unsigned, **£30–50/$45–75 (£150–200/$225–300 if perfect)**

Cut-steel beaded coin purse, c.1890, American, unsigned, **£15–30/$20–45**

▲ **Antique bargains**
While early bags can be very pricey, many humbler ones survive to expand your collection without costing the earth. This cut-steel coin purse is touchingly simple, well used, well loved and bound to appreciate in value.

Mesh bags

Metal mesh handbags first appeared in the mid-19thC and have gone in and out of fashion ever since. Reminiscent of the chainmail worn by medieval knights, these bags came in a variety of weights and weaves. The earliest examples were assembled painstakingly by hand and, as a consequence, tend to be made of larger links. The invention of a mesh-making machine in 1909, and later improvements to this technology in the 1920s, meant that superfine meshes became possible. The 1920s and 1930s are considered a highpoint for mesh and therefore special bags from this time are particularly sought after. Mesh bags must always be stored flat because if the mesh is bent it can then snap.

Silver-mesh bag, c.1910, American, signed "sterling – R+B.Co.", **£100–150/ $150–225**

▼ **Silver mesh**
The sterling mark on this bag indicates that it is made of silver. The box-chain handle, etched frame and faux sapphire clasp add value, while the name of the owner is charmingly engraved inside. The bag would, however, be more valuable if it had a pointed, gothic-style frame.

▲ **Vermeil**
Gold-tone mesh is often made of vermeil (silver-gilt). An elaborately decorated clasp, particularly with paste or precious stones, increases value. An unfortunate tear in the body reduces the value of this example.

Art Nouveau mesh bag, c.1900, probably European, unsigned, **£220–300/ $330–450**

• Examine mesh bags
with a magnifier. Marks
can be microscopic.
• Base-metal bags tend
to be heavy for their
size and links are larger.
• American silver bags
are usually stamped
"sterling"; European
ones say "silver", "925"
or bear silver hallmarks.
• Solid-gold mesh bags
are rare; look for carat
marks, jewelled clasps
and seed-pearl fringing.

▼ Early mesh

Early mesh is heavy and the individual links are obvious. This type can be less valuable, but here an interesting fleur-de-lis lid backed with a leaded mirror gives added interest. These bags are often made of base metal, so check carefully for rust and corrosion.

Metal mesh bag, c.1880, probably European, unsigned, **£150–200/ $225–300**

Silver-mesh bag, 1920s, European, signed with hallmarks, **£400–500/$600–750**

▲ Quality mesh

The individual links of this solid-silver bag are difficult to distinguish, the superfine weave giving it the texture of fabric. Its shirred fringe is of similar quality. Value is further enhanced by the unusually large size (approx. 20 x 15cm/8 x 6in) and the fired jeweller's enamel on the lid.

▼ Mandalian bag

These pretty mesh bags, introduced by Turkish immigrant Shatiel Mandalia, were extremely popular in the 1920s and 1930s. The best examples employ brash Art Deco colouring in geometric, stylized designs. Similar bags are often referred to as "Mandalian" even if unsigned.

Art Deco bag, 1920s, American, signed "Mandalian MFG. Co.", **£200–250/ $300–375**

Whiting & Davis

Founded in Massachusetts in 1876 and still in business today, Whiting & Davis have reigned supreme as makers of mesh bags, and their products provide a comprehensive history of changing styles and tastes. Examples from the 19th and early 20thC are usually plain, while colourful meshes were popular in the 1920s and early 1930s. In the late 1930s, in response to a longing for Hollywood glamour, a series of special high-fashion bags was designed exclusively for the company by couturier legends Paul Poiret and Elsa Schiaparelli. Since the 1930s the company has produced its ever-popular fish-scale mesh, in which flat plates are applied to a framework of underlying rings to create a continuous metallic surface.

▶ **Dresden mesh**
This type of mesh is identified by its soft, impressionistic colouring. The Art Deco clasp and zig-zag fringe add value to this example. Abstract patterns are the most common, but figural, and in particular floral, designs can also be found. This bag retains its original silk lining, a rare survival as contact with metal often led to the deterioration of fabrics. Note that linings can make damage to mesh more difficult to spot.

Dresden mesh bag, late 1920s, American, signed "Whiting & Davis Co. Mesh bags", **£180–200/ $270–300**

▼ **Flappers**
Plain and coloured metal meshes were a popular alternative to the ubiquitous beaded "flapper bags" of the 1920s. Make sure that chain handles match the metal of the frame, as replacement handles detract from value.

Dresden mesh bag, 1920s, American, signed "Whiting & Davis mesh bags Co. Reg. U.S. and Can.", **£120–140/ $180–210**

Assessing mesh
Damage is difficult
to spot when a bag
is closed. If a bag is
unlined, holes and weak
areas will become
apparent when you look
inside. The edges where
the mesh meets the
clasp are vulnerable,
particularly at the
corners; even small
separations will worsen.
Look out for repairs
with thread or wire.

Butterfly mesh bag, 1930s,
American, signed "Whiting
& Davis co. Mesh Bags",
£125–150/$185–225

▲ **"Bead-lite**
While most colourful mesh
bags have a smooth surface,
here each link is raised and
feels like a metal bead.
Advertised as "bead-lite" this
new style was billed as "chip
resistant", which unfortunately
it was not. Check condition
carefully; this example has
damage that lowers its value.

▼ **Post-war mesh**
Whiting & Davis
are best known
for their plain-
metal fish-scale
mesh in silver and gold
tones. Although first
made in the 1930s,
most notably for
bags designed by
Elsa Schiaparelli, it
took off in the 1950s.

Chainmail clutch bag,
1950s, American, signed "Whiting
& Davis Co.", **£50–75/$75–110**

Chainmail bag, late 1940s,
American, signed "Whiting &
Davis Co. Mesh bags. Made in
U.S.A.", **£150–200/$225–300**

▲ **Clasps**
While this later style of mesh
is not generally as valuable as
many earlier forms, it is now
highly collectable. Jewelled
clasps such as this one are rare
and sought after, but a soiled
or torn lining will detract from
value. A box bag in this mesh
is also a good find.

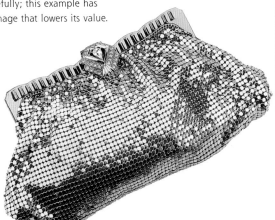

Art Deco

The conservative Edwardian lifestyle was swept away after World War I, replaced by a roller-coaster of fast women, fast cars, jazz clubs and Art Deco. This new style banished the fussy sentimentality of Art Nouveau in favour of a bolder and more modern look. Objects were flattened, streamlined and expressed in stylish geometric shapes. The 1920s flapper was the perfect sartorial expression of the Art Deco aesthetic. While Edwardian ladies were curvaceous and frilly, the flapper was long and lean. The writer Aldous Huxley described her as: "angular and tubular like a section of a boa constrictor dressed in clothes that emphasized this serpentine slimness". Her waistless dresses and crisp, bobbed hair required bolder, less overtly feminine, bags.

▲ Clutches

While many Art Deco bags are now very expensive, plainer leather or cloth versions make good buys for the collector on a budget. Clutch styles first became popular in the 1920s, so even simple examples such as this one mark an interesting place in handbag history. The geometric shapes here are typically Deco in style.

Leather clutch bag, late 1920s, English, unsigned, **£45–65/ $65–95**

▼ Jewelled clasps

The value of an Art Deco evening bag is often determined by the quality of its clasp. The best ones have precious or semi-precious stones in sharply contrasting colours. This green, black and silver combination is typical, but look out for burnt orange, black and silver, too. Settings can be smooth and unfaceted, as here, or carved to resemble flowers and leaves – a style popularized by Cartier in the 1920s.

Satin bag with jet, marcasite and chrysoprase set on a silver clasp, 1920s, probably French, unsigned, **£350–450/ $525–675**

Typical 1920s Art Deco motifs make a bag more valuable. Look out for:
• locusts, scarabs, greyhounds, gazelles, ships, cars, flower baskets, Jazz Age dancers, stylized female figures, especially nudes, and anything Egyptian.
• zig-zags, chevrons and repeating patterns, with contrasting colours.

▼ Enamel clasps

Enamel was the ideal medium for the flattened, stylized Deco look, and bags such as this one are highly sought after. Valuable "real" enamel, made by jewellers, has a glassy, translucent finish, while painted imitations appear chalky and opaque. Although very rare, look out for Deco bags by LaCloche, Mauboussin and Chaumet; these are usually of museum quality.

Satin bag with silver enamelled clasp, 1920s, French, unsigned, **£350–400/$525–600**

Celluloid vanity case, 1920s, French, unsigned, **£250–300/$375–450**

▲ Vanity cases

While Victorian and Edwardian ladies used make-up sparingly, and then only covertly, the 1920s flapper had no such inhibitions. There was a craze at this time for tasselled vanity cases on long silken cords. This one has an interior powder puff, mirror and lipstick holder. Celluloid, bakelite and tortoiseshell examples are all highly collectable.

▼ Beading

Beaded bags were perfect for jazzy, beaded flapper dresses, and the sentimental patterns of the early 20thC were updated to reflect the new Art Deco sensibility. The value of this bag is increased by its large size (25 x 15cm/ 10 x 6in) and its unusually wide wrist strap.

Beaded bag, 1920s, French, signed "Made in France", **£300–400/$450–600**

Screen gems & wartime shortages

In the 1930s fashion tired of the boyish, rather androgynous flapper silhouette and Hollywood stars such as Greta Garbo and Jean Harlow displayed curve after curve in glamorous, bias-cut evening gowns that fitted like a second skin. Shimmering bead, sequin and mesh handbags completed the more seductive look. This fashion extravaganza came to an abrupt halt in 1939 with the outbreak of World War II. Leather, cloth, metal and other traditional materials were now rationed and handbag designers looked to surprising new materials, while many women made their own bags or reused old ones.

▼ **Cordé bag**
These fabric bags were made of a twine-like cord and are usually found as clutches in envelope or fan shapes. The value of this example is greatly increased by a finely carved and tinted lucite frame. Metal was scarce during the war so bakelite and lucite plastics were used instead, particularly in costume jewellery and bag decoration.

Cordé and lucite bag, 1940s, American, signed "Genuine Cordé", **£150–250/ $225–375**

Enamel and fabric evening bag, late 1930s, English, unsigned, **£50–75/$75–110**

▲ **Double-hinged frames**
Frames hinged on four sides open out to form a square. This novelty device, introduced in Paris around the turn of the century, was used right up to the 1950s. Glittering fabric woven with metallic thread was particularly popular in the flashy 1930s.

Diamanté, velvet and satin clutch, date unknown, American, signed "Martin Van Schaak", **£150–250/ $225–375**

▲ Martin Van Schaak
This bag was made by Martin Van Schaak, one of New York's most exclusive purveyors of fine handbags. Too rarefied to operate from anything as public as a showroom, he preferred to call on his society clientele in their own homes. Any bag that bears his name is a fortuitous find.

▼ South America
Brazilian singer and comic actress Carmen Miranda sparked a craze in the 1940s for fashions and accessories from "South of the Border". Bags from these countries were, happily, unaffected by wartime restrictions. The dolls on this kitschy example wear miniature straw hats and carry wooden guitars.

Handmade cloth bag, 1940s, South American, unsigned, **£40–50/$60–75**

Coiled-plastic bag, 1940s, American, unsigned, **£75–95/$110–140**

▲ "Telephone wire" bag
These zany and colourful 1940s bags look as though they are made of coiled telephone wire. They came in a variety of shapes and styles, but this boxy type is the most collectable. Look out for similar bags made from large plastic tiles.

▼ Python

Python-skin bags are easily identified by their characteristic two-tone patterning, which was usually left in its natural state. Other species of snakeskin were commonly dyed in a range of colours. The chunky brass clasp and boxy shape of this bag date it to the 1940s.

Python bag, 1940s, American, unsigned, **£140–160/$210–240**

Tooled-leather bag and matching wallet, late 1940s, American, unsigned, **£90–110/$135–165**

▲ Tooled leather

Hand-tooled leather bags first appeared in about 1900 and were made up to the 1970s. The best early examples reflect contemporary decorative trends such as Arts and Crafts, Art Nouveau and Art Deco. This floral pattern was firmly established by the 1940s and remained popular until the 1960s. Look out for tooled bags signed "Rycroft".

▼ "Make do and mend"

The World War II "make do and mend" campaign urged women to create their own clothing and accessories from whatever spare material they could find. Handbags were made from dishtowels, draperies, fabric remnants or unwearable garments. This bag was originally a beaded dress, and closes with a reused 1930s diamanté clip.

Handmade beaded bag, mid-1940s, American, unsigned, **£30–50/$45–75**

Utility fashion
During World War II manufacturers could only produce items that conformed to strict government rules on colouring, length, fastenings and trims. This British "utility mark" showed that the standard had been met.

▼ Suede
Suede bags were popular during the 1930s and early 1940s. These came as simple envelope clutches, or in more interesting and collectable saucer, triangle and fan shapes. Boxy examples were common. Look out for Surrealist-inspired bags signed by Elsa Schiaparelli – these are now museum pieces.

Suede bag, early 1940s, American, signed "Dorian", **£30–50/$45–75**

Leather, chrome and bakelite clutch, 1930s, English, unsigned, **£175–275/$260–410**

▲ Canine collectables
The Scottish terrier as a decorative motif is associated with the 1930s, just as the greyhound conjures up the Art Deco '20s and the French poodle was the epitome of 1950s kitsch. The terrier here is made of carved bakelite, which is always a good feature on bags of this period.

Sequin evening bag, 1930s, French, signed "Made in France", **£60–80/$90–120 (bag), £500–700/$750–1,050 (complete set)**

▲ Sequins
This bag is part of a sequin evening set that includes a slinky, bias-cut dress, a shoulder cape and a matching hat. Sequins were widely used in the 1950s, but these small ones indicate that the bag is of an earlier date.

1930s–1950s: box bags

The 1920s vanity case was an early prototype for the larger box bag that emerged in the 1930s and has been with us ever since. These were certainly carried like ordinary handbags, but they also doubled as ornaments for display, especially on vanity tables where they served to store costume jewellery and make-up. The decorative appeal of vintage box bags is one of the reasons why they are particularly collectable today. The 1950s was a high point in box-bag design, and plastic pieces from this era are now highly sought after. Look inside for a maker's label or a mark incised on the hinge, and remember to check for cracking, which lowers value. These beautiful bags are far more fragile than they look.

▼ **Plastic boxes**
Plastic box bags were enormously popular in the 1950s and came in such a wide range of shapes and styles that some collectors focus entirely on these. Although brown is not the most sought-after colour, the value of this bag is enhanced by its carved bakelite lid and unusual, ribbed sides. Look out for bags signed "Rialto", "Llewellyn" or "Willardy"; these are all top-quality manufacturers.

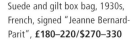
Suede and gilt box bag, 1930s, French, signed "Jeanne Bernard-Parit", **£180–220/$270–330**

▲ **Compact boxes**
This suede evening box bag has a two-part lid. The upper section functions as a compact, complete with mirror and swansdown powder puff. Value here is enhanced by the interesting curved shape and pristine condition.

Plastic box bag, 1950s, American, signed "Willardy", **£200–300/ $300–450**

The nose knows
Smell the inside of a plastic box before you buy, and avoid making the purchase if it exudes a strong, chemical odour. This means that it has been poorly manufactured or wrongly stored and is entering an irreversible process of decay that will lead to cracking and discoloration.

Gilt-metal box bag, 1950s, American, signed "Dorset Rex 5th Avenue", **£90–110/$135–165**

▲ **Metal boxes**
Woven-metal box bags from the 1950s are usually less valuable than plastic or beaded ones, but they are still very collectable. These came in gold, silver or a combination of the two. Check condition carefully, as scratches, dents and ill-fitting lids detract from value.

▼ **Beaded boxes**
Collectors love beaded box bags, but round or rectangular shapes are preferred. This one would also be worth more if it had bakelite decoration or a fancier metal frame. Look out for boxes made of iridescent blue "carnival" beads, signed "Fre-Mor".

Beaded box bag, late 1940s, American, signed "DuBonnette", **£100–150/$150–225**

Plastic and brass bag, 1950s, American, signed "Willardy", **£275–375/$410–560**

▲ **Better boxes**
The most valuable plastic boxes have a little something extra. Good features include inset fake jewels, embedded glitter, handpainted scenes and intricate metal overlays. The rarest colours are pale blue, yellow, jade green and red. Brown, pearlized white and grey are more common.

1900–1950: needlework

As women's roles changed and modern forms of entertainment emerged in the 20th century, needlework became a less popular pastime. There was still a taste, however, for needlework bags, but these were increasingly produced by specialist manufacturers. Austria has long been a centre for fine needlepoint and petit-point evening bags, where scenes taken from classical paintings and prints were copied in watercolour onto cardboard grids. Professional embroiderers then transferred those scenes, stitch by stitch, onto a delicate gauze backing, using up to 500 shades of silk thread and several thousand stitches per inch. Such bags were sold at justifiably high prices, and vintage examples are similarly sought after and expensive today. Less ambitious projects were usually homemade or mass-produced. All forms of needlework bags can be collectable, but values vary widely.

◀ **Petit point**

These petit-point bags were popular from the turn of the century right through to the 1950s. Collectors love this fine, detailed work and rate figural scenes such as this one more highly than simple, floral designs. These bags were rarely produced at home. Most originated in the specialist workshops of Austria and France. Pretty jewelled or enamel frames – this one uses pearl and enamel – enhance the value of bags that survive in good condition. Watch out for printed cloth imitations of petit point.

Evening bag,
c.1910,
Austrian,
unsigned,
**£300–500/
$450–750**

▼ **Domestic needlepoint**

This needlepoint sewing bag was made at home by its original owner and is perhaps a portrait of a favourite pet. Charming subjects, especially animals, add value to needlework products, although the plain, rather crude wooden handle here slightly detracts from the value.

Wood and
needlepoint
sewing bag,
date unknown,
English,
unsigned,
**£80–100/
$120–150**

Identifying needlework
Study fabrics with a magnifying glass (jeweller's loupe) if possible. In true needlework each stitch should be slightly raised and individual, like a tiny cloth bead. In fakes, the design is created by long, coloured threads that run continuously across the bag's surface.

▼ Fake needlework
Watch out for mass-produced handbags made to look like hand-sewn needlework. Some examples are collectable today, but they are worth far less than the real thing. Colour on fakes is usually brighter and more garish, and colour contrasts are jarring and sharp rather than subtly shaded. Also, fabrics tend to be stiffer.

Mass-produced fabric clutch, 1970s, American, signed with a patent number, **£20–30/$30–45**

Needlework bag, 1950s, American, unsigned, **£30–50/$45–75**

▲ Monogrammed bags
This home-made needlework sampler is finished off with a pair of shop-bought handles. The appearance of the original owner's initials on the outside of any style of handbag always lowers the value considerably, but an interior monogram makes little or no difference to the price.

▼ Commercial needlepoint
While this needlepoint floral pattern could date from almost any period, the shape of the handbag places it firmly in the 1950s. Its fine leather trim and interior indicate that it was commercially produced by a high-quality manufacturer.

Needlepoint bag, 1950s, Belgian, signed "Walborg Original", **£100–120/$150–180**

Post-war chic

Shortages persisted in Europe after the end of World War II, but for many, especially in the USA, the 1950s was a time of optimism and prosperity. The post-war period exploded in a riot of new products and a frenzy of retail therapy, and fashion was an obvious outlet. Christian Dior's "New Look" collection in 1947 satisfied a long-suppressed craving for overt femininity and, perhaps most exciting of all, featured dresses that required acres of previously rationed fabric. These called for an array of appropriate accessories, and the 1950s emerged as the golden age of fashion extras. Costume jewellery, shoes, gloves and handbags were produced in an unprecedented range.

▼ Confetti
Early evening bags had tended towards luxury materials, but the 1950s spirit of innovation and novelty allowed plastic to come out at night. Here a confetti of plastic pieces is welded together to form a rigid clutch purse. Such bags are fragile and are therefore rare on today's market. They should be used and stored carefully.

Gold patent-leather envelope bag, 1950s, American, unsigned, **£25–35/$35–50**

Pastel plastic clutch bag, 1950s, American, unsigned, **£75–85/$110–125**

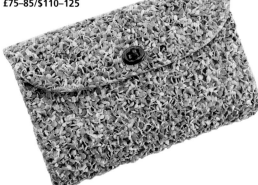

▲ Gold rush
Strict rules applied to 1950s fashion: the cocktail dress was quite distinct from the dinner dress, and satin and brocade could not be worn in any style before 6pm. Outfits also had to co-ordinate perfectly. Nothing could, perhaps, be safer than the gold envelope, which was available in leather, cloth and plastic versions.

Fashion designers
Many wonderful bags
are anonymous creations,
but look out for signed
pieces by legendary
designers such as
Balenciaga, Givenchy
or Dior, which were
sold in department
stores and upmarket
boutiques. The designer's
name may be on a label
sewn inside the bag, or
stamped on the lining.

FACT FILE

Dewdrop bag, 1950s, American,
signed "Lumuned Cordé Bead",
£20–40/$30–60

▼ Matched sets

The fashion rules and
formalities of the 1950s
meant that dressing properly
sometimes felt like hard work.
Matched sets were a welcome
relief. This satin bag and
stiletto (spike-heeled shoe)
set is highly collectable –
a quintessential slice of
fashion history. Look out for
sets in lucite or reptile skin,
as these are the most valuable.

Butterfly-print satin shoes
and handbag, 1950s,
American, signed
"Reeves",
**£90–100/
$135–150**

▲ Plastic beads

Simple, unadorned gold
and silver bags were
enormously popular for
evening wear, but they
could not satisfy the restless
1950s fashion imagination
on their own. For the slightly
more adventurous, this hinged
cloth bag has clear-plastic beads
that shimmer like dewdrops.
Look out for brightly coloured
versions of this style.

Pearl and rhinestone clutch,
1950s, Hong Kong, signed "Made
in Hong Kong", **£18–30/$25–45**

▲ Pearls

While glittering rhinestones
reigned supreme in the
fabulous '50s, faux pearls also
held their own, and appeared
not only on jewellery but also
on clothing and bags. These
little clutches are easy to find
today and prices are low. Their
interest to collectors lies in the
variety of shapes and styles,
but check condition carefully.

Gold patent-leather evening bag, 1950s, probably Czech, unsigned, **£200–250/$300–375**

▲ Antique look

This bag recalls an earlier era, and may in fact incorporate an older Czech clasp, reused and updated in the 1950s with a new patent-leather body. The clasp has semi-precious stones set on gold-plated metal. Similar clasps are occasionally made of solid gold or platinum, with precious gems. Check for carat marks (such as 14k or 22k), on the inside and the outside.

▼ Beading

Beaded bags were revived in the 1950s and a now highly collectable range came from Hong Kong. The best bags feel heavy for their size. They bear a long, hinged, metal clasp, beaded on the outside with punctured holes underneath. This combination of beading and needlework adds value to the bag.

Beaded and petit-point bag, 1950s, Hong Kong, signed "Kishu's East–West Fashions. Hong Kong", **£200–300/$300–450**

▼ Other decorations

Beads and rhinestones were not the only materials used for decoration. Here pieces of branch coral have been painted and then sewn onto a silver cloth bag in a sea fan design, which is carefully outlined in metallic cord. Such unique, labour-intensive bags are a collector's dream.

Cloth, coral and silk-lined evening bag, 1950s, probably French, unsigned, **£80–120/$120–180**

Gilt-metal *minaudière*, 1950s, American, signed *"Evans"*, **£120–140/$180–210**

▲ The *minaudière*

Cosmetics were scarce during wartime, but they returned with a vengeance in the 1950s and bags responded accordingly. This bag is, in fact, a hand-held compact, with room inside for a variety of evening necessities. It is an updated version of the metal vanity case, or *minaudière*, invented by French jewellers Van Cleef and Arpels in the 1930s.

▶ Inside story

The interior of a *minaudière* is divided into compartments for lipstick, powder, money and cigarettes. Plain metal examples are more common than this one, which is made of satin and rhinestones. A small battery-operated light mounted below the mirror is a special feature that adds value. Broken or foxed mirrors detract from value, while unused *minaudières* command the best prices.

Evening *minaudière*, 1950s, French, signed "Boite de Nuit. Werber. Paris", **£180–200/$270–300**

1950s: daytime bags

In the 1950s a boom in handbag sales in the USA meant that the average American woman bought more new handbags in that decade than most of us today will buy in a lifetime, so plenty survive to amuse and enchant. In fact, there are so many to find that some collectors confine themselves to this period alone. Daytime bags were produced in an astonishing variety of shapes, sizes and styles. While the decade leaned towards a busy, "more is more" mentality, a parallel aesthetic of pared-down minimalism also flourished. This was helped along by society's enthusiasm for science and technology. Designers created futuristic furniture that would have looked at home in a spaceship, and this style soon appeared in clothing and handbags.

▼ Canvas

Not all 1950s bags are inordinately expensive, and plenty of practical and affordable examples can be found at fairs and markets. Totes such as these will never be very valuable but they are prettier and more fun than many modern examples. Look out for cloth, wicker and plastic versions. Those printed with typical 1950s motifs are particularly collectable.

Matching pair of floral canvas totes, 1950s, American, unsigned, **£15–20/ $20–30**

Cloth bag, 1950s, American, unsigned, **£50–70/ $75–105**

▲ Feminine designs

Brocaded cloth bags were popular in floral, abstract or, more rarely, figural designs. Such bags are not true needlework but use machine-made fabrics. The value of this one is increased by its figural subject, pristine condition and deep pile.

Collectors prize the kitschier themes in 1950s fashion and design, as they date a handbag and increase its value. Look out for:

- French poodles
- masks
- harlequins
- playing cards
- ballerinas
- Parisian landmarks
- sealife
- Venetian scenes

Burlap bag, 1950s, American, signed "Hand decorated original by Caron of Houston", **£95–115/$140–170**

▲ Collage culture

Collage was a popular technique for decorating handbags in the 1950s, for both day and evening styles. Here glass beads, metallic lace and tinted velvet are combined in a highly collectable "ripe-peach" design. Collage bags are usually hand decorated.

▼ Kitsch collectables

The decade's longing for glamour found expression in its love affair with France. The French poodle was a favourite theme, starting as a symbol of sophistication and ending up as an icon of the kitschier side of 1950s style.

Collage poodle bag with beads, glitter and snail shells, 1950s, American, signed "la franca", **£160–190/$240–285**

Straw bag with beads, glitter and brass, 1950s, Belgian, signed "Walborg handmade", **£120–150/$180–225**

▲ City baskets

Cloth and leather were favoured for day bags, but straw was also popular. Such expensive, high-quality examples as this one were not intended for the beach. Check that decorations are intact as missing pieces are difficult to replace and lower the value.

Matt vinyl "space age" bag, 1950s, American, signed "Melbourne bags", **£60–80/$90–120**

▲ Vinyl

The enthusiasm for synthetic materials in the 1950s meant that a unique, well-made vinyl handbag was more desirable than an ordinary leather one. This bag rests on brass feet, which can be an indicator of quality. Be careful how you wear and store plastic handbags, especially vinyls, as they scratch and dent easily.

▼ Sleek chic

Proud to be plastic, this glossy vinyl bag steers clear of fussy decoration and favours clean lines and a sharply defined architectural shape. A far cry from its collage contemporaries, it is equally prized for its bold, futuristic design. Look out for this style in rounded or oval shapes. Red is the most sought-after colour.

Glossy vinyl "space age" bag, 1950s, American, signed "Fabriget. Made in U.S.A.", **£130–150/$195–225**

Brass and leather travelling bag, 1950s, American, signed "Prestige", **£220–250/ $330–375**

▲ "La dolce vita"

The era's romance with all things European is evident in this high-quality leather travelling bag. Its decorative brass plate is inscribed with the names of the 1950s' swankiest resorts, while its rather incongruous design, based on a man's business briefcase, stylishly undercuts its reference to fun in the sun.

FACT FILE

New materials
Synthetic fabrics and
plastics, developed by
necessity in World War II,
were explored purely for
fun in the 1950s. Early
plastic handbags are
highly collectable, but
beware of faults caused
by the new technology;
cracking and peeling is
usually irreparable and
will lower value.

▼ Modern tapestry
In this bag
two seemingly
contradictory strands of 1950s
design work happily together.
Machine-made fabric, harking
back to antique tapestries,
is combined with vinyl in
a simple, modern silhouette.
As with all cloth bags, but
particularly tapestries and
brocades, watch out for fraying,
especially at the corners.

Tapestry bag, 1950s, American,
unsigned, **£75–95/$110–140**

Burlap insect bag, 1950s,
American, signed "Roger van S.",
£100–120/$150–180

▲ Surrealism
The 1950s' love of novelty
created a taste for witty,
almost surreal combinations
reminiscent of fashion
designer Elsa Schiaparelli's
work in the 1930s. Here brass
butterflies and horseflies
cavort on a field of natural
burlap piped in shiny black
plastic. Roger van S. bags tend
to be unusual and
highly prized.

▼ More dash than cash
Elegant and expensive vinyl
bags were de rigueur for even
the dressiest occasions, but
women, especially teenagers,
often felt the need for
humbler, roomier, more
practical designs. Special
bags and cases for bowling,
records, make-up and even
dolls survive from this period.

Red vinyl bag, 1950s, English,
unsigned, **£40–60/$60–90**

Novelties

Novelty bags come in unusual shapes, or function in unexpected ways. Some of the earliest and best were made to complement Elsa Schiaparelli's Surrealist-inspired fashion of the 1930s, but these were made in very limited editions and remain extremely rare today. The 1950s' love of gadgetry and witty, tongue-in-cheek accessories launched novelty bags into the mainstream, and many good examples survive from this period. The 1960s also produced a rich vein of handmade examples. An interest in novelty continued to weave in and out of handbag design for the rest of the 20thC, finding contemporary expression in the work of modern designers such as Lulu Guinness (see p.57).

Bag with composition (clay/plaster) head, silk hair, felt and paper dress, 1950s, American, unsigned, **£60–90/$90–135**

▶ **Doll bags**
Beautiful women in the 1950s were called "dolls", so it is not surprising that dolls appear in the decorative vocabulary of handbags. This one's face is handpainted and she wears a felt dress trimmed with paper playing cards. The bag's tiny, zippered opening and cramped interior suggest that it was made for a child. It is highly kitsch, and highly collectable.

▼ **Figural bags**
Figural bags can be extremely valuable finds. A 1930s handbag shaped like a steamship, or a 1940s box bag depicting a bottle of champagne on ice, command four-figure sums at auction. This iconic poodle is another holy grail for collectors of novelty handbags.

Beaded poodle bag with rhinestone collar, 1950s, Belgian, signed "Walborg", **£1,000–1,200/$1,500–1,800**

FACT FILE

• Look out for rare 1930s surrealist bags shaped like lobsters, flowerpots, birdcages, snails and so on. Those signed "Schiaparelli" are museum pieces.
• Animal-shaped bags from all periods are sought after, especially *minaudières*.
• Bags with unexpected gadgetry, such as watches, barometers, music boxes or lights are all very collectable.

▼ Plastic box bags

This plastic handbag is shaped like a beehive and its carved bakelite lid is decorated with brass bees. Figurals are the rarest and most valuable of all plastic box bags, but beware as chemical deterioration seriously undermines value.

Bakelite and plastic box bag, 1950s, American, signed "Llewellyn", **£250–350/ $375–525**

Plastic telephone bag with original paper label, 1970s, American, signed "Dallas Handbags", **£250–350/ $375–525**

▲ Mobile phones

Artist Salvador Dalí transformed the telephone into a surrealist object when he substituted its handset for a plastic boiled lobster. He also designed a telephone-shaped handbag for Elsa Schiaparelli. This 1970s version goes a step further: when plugged into a wall socket it does in fact work – a forerunner of today's mobile phone.

▼ Time pieces

This bag features a battery-operated wallclock that can be removed from its zippered inner compartment. Identical modern clocks are inexpensive and widely available, so can easily be substituted if the clock stops working.

"Wetlook" vinyl clock bag, 1980s, American, signed "Marilyn Brooks", **£50–70/$75–105**

Exotic skins

While ordinary leather had long been a staple for everyday bags, manufacturers looked to more unusual species for their luxury creations. Special bags were made of ostrich, python, antelope and even sharkskin, but alligator and crocodile have remained the most popular of all these so-called "exotics". Crocodile and alligator skins are virtually indistinguishable, so value depends on the quality of the skin itself, and on the craftsmanship and condition of the handbag. Look for bags with a smooth glossy texture and avoid any that feel coarse or brittle. Dryness, peeling and cracking are common problems, even with quality bags if they have been stored improperly. Examine handles – particularly the vulnerable areas where they attach to the bag.

Crocodile bag, 1950s, American, signed "Escort", **£150–200/ $225–300**

▼ Classic croc

This simple 1950s crocodile handbag is a type that remains sought after today, partly because it is still so wearable. Shiny black and a variety of brown tones were the most popular colours, while maroon and green bring higher prices owing to their rarity. Watch out for ordinary leather that has been embossed to look like reptile skin.

▼ "Carry on" luggage

With the expansion of the railway network in the 19thC, these "Gladstone" or "doctor's" bags became popular travelling accessories for both men and women. The presence of a date and patent number on the clasp adds interest. Overly large and miniature versions bring the best prices. Check the condition of the bag carefully as this will affect value.

Alligator bag, late 19thC, English, unsigned, **£100–120/ $150–180**

Quality control
• Suede or leather linings and intricate metal slide-and-twist locks indicate quality.
• Plastic, felt or oilskin linings guarantee that a bag is poorly made.
• Check for signatures: Asprey and Cartier bags can be very valuable.
• Value can soar with the stamp "Hermès".

Alligator bag, 1950s, South American, unsigned, **£40–60/$60–90**

▲ Taxidermy
Leather-laced edges, a crude clip and a coarse thick texture suggest that this is a poor-quality bag. While some collectors will buy such bags as curiosities, the stuffed alligator lowers its value, perhaps by drawing attention to the harsh reality that underpins the production of bags with exotic skins. The presence of an animal's head or foot, even on an otherwise high-quality bag, considerably reduces value.

▼ Alligator skin
The slim, elegant silhouette and Art Deco brass edging greatly increase the value of this 1930s alligator bag. Bakelite and chrome details on clasps are also attractive to collectors. Unusual shapes, especially box bags, fetch the best prices, but as always condition is vital.

Alligator bag, 1930s, American, unsigned, **£200–300/$300–450**

Lizard bag, 1950s, American, signed "Bellestons", **£70–90/$105–135**

▲ Lizard
This high-quality bag is made of lizard skin – identifiable by its dense pattern of tiny scales. Crocodile and alligator skins tend to be more desirable, but value here is enhanced by the bag's pristine suede interior, which includes a lizard-trimmed mirror and matching coin purse.

1950–1970: status bags

In the period before World War II, expensive handbags tended to be more obvious, broadcasting their rarity with precious metals and glittering jewels. By the 1950s, however, there were more plain, understated styles, which could only be recognized by a wealthy and fashionable elite. Such "status" bags are high-quality, carefully crafted pieces, often produced by traditional leatherwork firms. Subtle details signal the value of these bags to those in the know. Hermès' padlock clasps, Chanel's "CC" and Gucci's trademark green and red stripe were part of a hidden language of symbols that only went public in the status-driven 1980s. Status bags have been widely faked, so buy with care. Charity-shop bargains may be worth the risk, but for top-price bags keep to reputable specialist dealers or auction houses.

Leather and gilt-chain bag, 1950s, French, signed "Chanel",
£250–350/
$375–525

▶ **Chanel 2:55**
Named after the date of its debut in February 1955, this quilted leather classic has been perennially popular. As a high-priced status bag it has also been widely copied. Genuine bags tend to be heavier than fakes; a leather-lined interior and Chanel signatures stamped on the catch and lining are also good indicators of authenticity.

▼ **Bonnie Cashin**
American fashion designer Bonnie Cashin made a range of leather handbags that have become highly collectable. Look out for her trademark metallic hardware in the form of chunky brass studs and twist-lock closures. A striped cloth lining is also typical.

Tote bag, c.1970s, American, signed "Bonnie Cashin"
£200–300/
$300–450

Identifying Kelly bags
Apart from the Hermès signature stamped inside, look out for the Kelly bag's distinctive metal-tipped clasp, which can be closed with a tiny padlock. A hidden key, sheathed in leather, often dangles from the handle. Kelly bags were made in crocodile, ostrich or plain leather.

▼ Hermès Kelly bags

The Kelly bag, named after Grace Kelly (Princess of Monaco), who often wore this style, has become a holy grail for handbag collectors. Vintage examples change hands for large amounts of money at top auction houses, so a bargain find is truly serendipitous, but watch out for fakes.

Crocodile Kelly bag, early 1960s, French, signed "Hermès, Paris", **£1,000–3,000/$1,500–4,500**

Leather and gold-plated bag, late 1960s, French, signed "Hermès, Paris", **£75–100/$110–150 (£400–500/$600–750 if perfect)**

▲ Hermès Constance bags

Hermès was founded in 1837 as a harness and saddle-maker, but as cars replaced horses the company shifted into the production of fine leather wallets and handbags. While the Kelly bag is the most sought after, all Hermès products are attractive to collectors. The Constance bag is easily identified by its gilt-metal "H" logo, but value here is greatly undermined by the missing handle.

▼ Gucci

Collectors love this classic Gucci bag, and its plain leather body and bamboo handle are good indicators that it is authentic. Fakes of this style were, in fact, rarely made. Logo-patterned canvas bags are a much riskier proposition, so purchase those with care (see pp.54–5).

Leather and bamboo bag, 1960s, Italian, signed "Gucci", **£150–250/$225–375**

Basket bags

Derived from the plain and practical straw shopping baskets that many women carried in the days before throwaway grocery bags, basket-style bags quickly left behind their humble origins and became highly decorative. Some handbag enthusiasts prefer to collect by category, and baskets are a popular choice because a wide variety of unique and attractive examples survive. These turn up on the vintage market at prices that are readily affordable. Many interesting baskets were made in the 1950s to accessorize casual summer outfits with a dash of Italian *dolce vita* spirit. The most collectable ones feature pretty, detailed decoration with shells, velvet, ribbons, silk flowers or wax fruit. Whether made of straw, wicker, rush or raffia, all baskets are fragile, so treat them with care.

Leather and straw bag, 1950s, Italian, signed "Made in Italy", **£75–95/ $110–140**

▼ Leather and straw
The earth-toned leather flowers on this unusual basket nicely complement the colour and texture of the woven-straw body. While most basket bags take this common, rectangular shape, look out for novelties; figural baskets, which were made in the shape of hats, umbrellas and animals, are highly collectable.

▲ Velvet fruit
This very collectable basket features velvet strawberries and peapods bursting with faux pearls. Identical decoration appears on 1950s cardigans and is equally prized by collectors of vintage clothing. Value here is reduced by damage to the wicker.

Wood, wicker and velvet bag, 1950s, American, unsigned, **£60–80/ $90–120**

Nantucket baskets
These bags, handmade for generations in Nantucket, Massachusetts, are now the most valuable and sought after of all vintage baskets. They have a tightly woven straw body and a wooden lid that is decorated with a carved ivory plaque. These carvings usually depict nautical subjects such as seashells, lighthouses and whales.

▼ **Collage baskets**
The velvet flowers and fruits on this painted wicker basket bag are typical of 1950s collage design. Although it looks homemade, this style was manufactured and was often sold in popular US resorts such as Miami or Palm Springs. Check condition carefully as cracked wicker, missing pieces of collage and unravelling handles all detract from value.

Wicker and velvet bag, 1950s, American, unsigned, **£75–95/$110–140**

Raffia basket, 1950s, American, unsigned, **£75–95/$110–140**

▲ **Sealife**
Baskets with a sealife theme are always popular with collectors. Most were made in the 1950s to accessorize casual summer fashion styles such as sundresses. This raffia example is decorated with pearls, real seashells, glass beads and silk and velvet flowers. Overall, this is a highly desirable bag.

▼ **Easter baskets**
Handmade by its original owner, this bag features a profusion of kitschy plastic flowers and velvet ribbon. Its wide weave is reminiscent of traditional Easter baskets and shopping baskets. The lace-trimmed, floral-cotton interior is another attractive feature.

Home-made bag, 1960s, American, unsigned, **£35–55/$50–80**

The swinging '60s

The 1960s fashion scene was characterized by a "youthquake" – a global style shift that rejected the 1950s grown-up look in favour of one that was decidedly younger and more fun. The first phase detonated on the King's Road and Carnaby Street in London, led by lifestyle icon and fashion designer Mary Quant. Bags made of plastic beads or shiny PVC typify this early phase. By the late 1960s, "youthquake" style started to look too much like the consumer-feeding frenzy of the 1950s, and London's shopaholic mods were replaced by the California hippies. Their preference for natural, handmade products is echoed in the macramé, embroidered and Indian-style handbags that were carried by both men and women.

▼ "Op Art"

The 1950s enthusiasm for synthetic materials turned into a love affair by the early 1960s, and this shiny "wet look" plastic was particularly popular. It was used not only for handbags and shoes but also for clothing. Value here is increased by a geometric, black and white "Op Art" design that typifies the early mod look.

Plastic bag, early 1960s, American, signed "Ingber", **£100–150/ $150–225**

Plastic tote, early 1960s, American, unsigned, **£40–60/$60–90**

▲ Plastic totes

Few 1960s plastic totes survive, so they are quite collectable today. Avoid storing PVC or printed plastics in other plastic material such as bubble wrap because surface treatments can fuse the materials together; always use tissue paper.

▼ **Shoulder straps**

Plastic was also a popular material for beaded bags. This one reflects the 1960s fashion for shoulder straps – a style that was now required for hands-free dancing at clubs and discos. Shoulder straps made from long, gilt chains were pioneered by Coco Chanel in the late 1950s, but these soon became mainstream and appear on all kinds of bags in the early 1960s.

Plastic and gilt bag, 1960s, American, unsigned,
£20–30/$30–45

Metal and leather bag, 1960s, French, interior metal plaque signed "Paco Rabanne",
£200–300/$300–450

▲ **Paco Rabanne**

This fashion designer was famous for his metal-disc dresses, which are worth a fortune on today's vintage market. His handbags are also valuable, but only when signed. Rabanne's style was widely copied by many lesser manufacturers and these mass-produced bags are not nearly as valuable as the real thing.

▼ **Natural materials**

In the mid-1960s the word "plastic" became a derogatory term: "plastic people" were false, materialistic types. The shift in attitude was reflected in various forms of fashion that now rejected synthetic materials in favour of natural products. This handbag is interesting as an early illustration of the new outlook. The style is that of earlier bags, but wooden beads replace plastic as the material of choice.

Wood-bead bag, mid-1960s, American, unsigned,
£20–30/$30–45

Suede and brass bag,
mid-1960s, American, unsigned,
£90–120/$135–180

▲ From mod to hippy

By the mid-1960s fashion
had lost its taste for synthetic
materials, and a wide range
of leather, suede, cotton and
rope handbags quickly came
to the fore. This mod, oversized,
metal-coil bag bridges the
stylistic gap between the early
and late years of the decade
and would, therefore, be
a fortunate find for any
1960s enthusiast.

▼ Ethnic styles

Cloth shoulder bags were
extremely popular in the
mid-1960s, and fringed
bottoms such as the one on
this bag became a typical
feature of the style. Look
out for heavily embroidered
versions, especially those with
inset mirrors. These bags were
often souvenirs of the "Hippy
Trail" of people visiting India.

Woven cloth shoulder bag,
1960s, American, unsigned,
£12–18/$18–27

Macramé rope and wood bag,
1960s, Philippine, signed "Mister
Ernest handbags inc. Made in
Philippines", **£20–40/$30–60**

▲ Macramé

The hippy living space, or
"pad", was not complete
without a collection of long
macramé plant holders
suspended from the ceiling.
These might contain anything
from spider plants and ferns
to illicit, home-grown
marijuana. Rope or jute
shoulder bags in a similar
style were equally popular,
and survive today to mark
this hippy love for natural,
handmade products.

Pucci bags
• The fabric of Pucci bags is signed; look for "Emilio" written as a black script signature.
• Bags should also be signed inside. Common marks include "Emilio Pucci" and "Emilio Pucci bags by Jana".
• Good condition is vital, as dry cleaning is rarely successful.

Plastic and cloth bag, 1970s, Hong Kong, signed "Made in Hong Kong", **£20–30/$30–45**

▲ Hippy fakes
Try not to confuse true 1960s hippy handbags with the mass-produced imitations that proliferated in the early 1970s. In this example, plastic beads have been glued by machine to waffle cotton, and a strip of ready-made fringe basted to the edge. Ironically, such bags have recently become collectable in their own right, but look out for more elaborate figural scenes; the cat and the fishbowl is proving a popular vintage design.

▼ From hippy to Pop Art
This is another interesting transitional bag, which combines hippy fringed suede and "flower power" motifs with a later, 1970s Pop Art aesthetic. Designers in the 1970s loved to include disembodied lips in their work – an idea that Prada recently revived in a fabric print as part of their millennium clothing collection.

Suede bag, early 1970s, American, unsigned, **£35–45/$50–65**

Silk, leather and gilt bag, 1960s, Italian, signed "Emilio Pucci. Italy", **£400–500/$600–750**

▲ Pucci
Italian fashion designer Emilio Pucci made some of the most sought after of all 1960s bags. The best ones feature silk or velvet exteriors in psychedelic prints. They often have top-quality kid-leather linings and trims in complementary jewel colours. Large bags in mint condition are the most valuable.

1960s: hobbies & crafts

The hippies' "do it yourself" approach to fashion trickled down to even the most conservative ladies during the 1960s, so that those who had opted out of the drug culture, the sexual revolution and the craze for the micro-mini skirt finally found a piece of the decade that they could call their own. Women set about making clothing, jewellery and handbags at home. Specialist hobby and craft shops proliferated in Britain and the USA, selling handbag-parts and kits, while some women preferred to decorate "found objects" such as tin pails and lunch boxes. Home-made bags from the 1960s do not yet command high prices, but the best ones are unique, highly personal creations, and prices for these have already started to rise.

▼ **Enid Collins**
Jewelled box bags by Collins of Texas are highly sought after and come in a wide variety of sizes and designs. Some collectors focus entirely on these particular bags. This one is signed inside "Original Box Bag by Collins of Texas", and has an "EC" monogram on the exterior.

Wood and paste "Papillon" bag, 1960s, American, **£70– 100/ $105–150**

Stiffened cloth and vinyl bag, 1960s, American, **£50–75/$75–110**

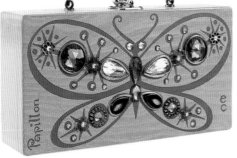

▲ **Collins cloth**
Cloth Collins bags are slightly less valuable than wooden versions but good designs still fetch good prices. This bag is signed; look for the "EC" monogram on the outside, which refers to the owner and designer, Enid Collins.

Découpage

In découpage, images are cut out and glued onto a handbag – usually wooden – and then protected with a layer of clear shellac. Magazines in the 1960s provided a steady stream of free pictures, but serious enthusiasts chose theirs from the huge variety on sale in most local hobby shops.

▼ Detachable bag covers

The 1960s saw the debut of the wooden-handled bag with detachable covers. Women who did craftwork bought these special handles (fitted with a row of buttons) and then made a variety of covers, to suit different outfits. This style continued to be popular in the "preppy" years of the late 1970s and early 1980s.

"Flower power" bag, late 1960s, American, unsigned, **£15–25/$20–35**

Découpage wooden box, 1960s, American, **£85–110/$125–165**

▲ Découpage

For those who did not have the time or inclination to make bags at home, handmade products could be bought at craft fairs or charity events. This découpage bag, signed "Handcrafted by the Friends of the Open Door", was sold to benefit a dog shelter, and the original owner has mounted a photo of her own pet inside.

▼ Transfers ("decals")

In the crafts-mad 1960s, plastic transfers, known as "decals" in the USA, were an incredibly popular decoration for antique trunks, mailboxes, milk-cans and home-made handbags. Here an ordinary metal lunchbox has been painted, adorned with decals and then varnished with shellac. A floral cotton interior and ribbon-wrapped handle finish it off.

Lunchbox bag, late 1960s, American, unsigned, **£25–35/$35–50**

The 1970s

The 1970s are best remembered for platform shoes and bell-bottom trousers, but such excesses obscure the fact that many different looks coexisted. For most of the decade the fashion press wondered if the 1970s had started yet. This indecision produced a rich variety of handbags. The hippy hang-over meant that ethnic styles persisted, but they were now mass produced in plastic and PVC. David Bowie and the "glam rockers" rejected hippy grunge in favour of flashy gold lamé, sequins and glitter – a theme that was continued in disco bags. Fashion designer Halston cultivated a stark minimalism based on plain jersey dresses, while Yves St Laurent promoted crisp trouser-suits for women with masculine tailoring, both of which called for chic, clutch-style bags.

Leather shoulder bag, 1970s, Mexican, signed "Hecho en Mexico for Rosas", **£20–30/ $30–45**

▲ **Embossed leather**
The hippy shoulder bag continued into the 1970s, and embossed leather versions, handmade in the USA or Mexico, were hugely popular. The flower design and toggle closure here are typical features. Such bags are not very collectable at present, but with recent revivals of interest in 1970s fashion, prices are rising.

▼ **The jeans bag**
Denim continued to be popular, but its contact with the mainstream and the 1970s' kitsch aesthetic meant that it ended up with designer logos or in cute new guises that would have horrified the hard-core hippy. Most 1970s denim bags were commercially manufactured, but some were made at home from an unwanted pair of old jeans. This bag is a fun souvenir of the decade.

Denim jeans bag, 1970s, American, unsigned, **£20– 30/ $30–45**

Leather and snakeskin clutch, 1970s, Italian, unsigned, **£40–60/$60–90**

▲ Return of the clutch

The clutch bag virtually disappeared in the swinging '60s, but it came back in force in the 1970s and was favoured by the decade's sharp dressers. Here black patent leather is decorated with a pastel collage of leather and snakeskin in a typical Pop Art-style design. Always store snakeskin in tissue paper because its scales can fuse to bubble wrap and other types of plastic sheeting.

▼ The magazine clutch

Elsa Schiaparelli pioneered the use of reading matter as fashion with her 1930s newsprint handbags and neckties. This later incarnation features a rigid plastic clutch in the form of a folded magazine. Various magazine covers were used for this '70s classic, but value depends entirely on condition.

Magazine clutch, 1970s, China, signed "Mister Ernest Handbags inc. Made in China", **£45–65/$70–95**

Suede clutch, 1970s, English, signed "Jean Muir", **£130–180/$195–270**

▲ Designer bags

Leather and suede cut-outs were a popular decorative motif in the decade. Look out for quality bags by designers such as Halston and Yves St Laurent. Their 1970s clothing and accessories have now made the "A list" with cutting-edge fashion collectors. This suede clutch is by English designer Jean Muir, another hot name on today's vintage market.

The 1980s

During most of the 1990s everyone tried to forget about shoulder pads, logo dressing and batwing sleeves, but in the early 21stC the 1980s have enjoyed a huge revival with the fashion cognoscenti, and original handbags from that decade are now hot property on the vintage market. Go for logo-patterned designer styles, but watch out for fakes. Many genuine logo bags are simply plastic-coated canvas and are therefore easier to copy than hand-sewn leather styles. Because they are still hugely popular, there is a thriving trade in counterfeit products. Other fashionable looks include satchel shapes, called "doctor's bags", and over-the-top leather pieces that express the 1980s' "more is more" mentality.

Leather and canvas satchel, 1980s, French, signed "Louis Vuitton. Made in France", **£150–250/ $225–375**

▼ Louis Vuitton
The man behind these bags, Louis Vuitton, was originally a luggage packer for wealthy families in mid-19thC France. He then opened his own firm and manufactured suitcases and trunks decorated with the distinctive "LV" logo pattern that is still used today. By the 20thC the company had turned to handbags, and these became universally popular in the 1980s.

▲ Christian Dior
Dior logo-patterned clothing and accessories first appeared in the 1950s and then enjoyed a huge vogue in the status-driven 1980s. The look was revived again in the early 21stC by Dior designer John Galliano, and therefore dating such pieces can be extremely difficult.

Canvas and leather satchel, 1980s, French, signed "Christian Dior", **£120–170/$180–255**

▼ Real or fake?

Prices for expensive logo bags have risen in response to mainstream fashion, but will fall when the logo trend passes. Distinguishing genuine logo bags from high-quality imitations is fiendishly difficult. To check authenticity look inside: the interior should be leather or suede. Also examine trims and straps: if stitches are unravelling, the bag is probably a fake. Inside this genuine Gucci bag is a leather tab stamped with a unique number. Plain leather Gucci bags are also collectable and, happily, less often faked.

Cloth, gilt and leather bag, 1980s, Italian, signed "Gucci. Made in Italy", **£150–250/$225–375**

Metal and paste *minaudière*, 1980s, American, signed "Judith Leiber", **£1,000–1,500/$1,500–2,250**

▲ Judith Leiber

Collectors love Judith Leiber's *minaudière* evening bags. Figural styles such as this one are the most sought after and valuable. The best examples are studded with up to 10,000 hand-set Swarovski paste stones in a subtly graded carpet of continuous colour.

▼ Characteristic creations

As well as logo and designer bags, some anonymous creations can be collectable if they express a strong 1980s trend. Flashy gold or silver leather is good, especially when jazzed-up with fake stones, bows or other fussy detail. Bags decorated with scrunched-up leather flowers are highly sought after by today's 1980s dressers.

Leather bag, 1980s, Italian, signed "Made in Italy", **£50–70/$75–105**

Future collectables

The late 1990s and early 21stC have been a great era for handbags, so start your collection now! Key looks include eccentric one-off bags that are utterly impractical but so delightful that this does not matter. These are often inspired by vintage bags, just as the vintage look has underpinned clothing styles since the late 1990s. The logo craze is another significant element, fuelled by young designers such as Tom Ford at Gucci and Marc Jacobs at Louis Vuitton, who have breathed new life into these classic brands. Prada and Fendi are also big contemporary names and their 21stC bags have become instant collectables. Dress agencies report that a good designer bag holds its value far better than a piece of clothing.

Leather "bowling bag", c.2000, Italian, signed "Prada", **£150–250/ $225–375 (second hand)**

▼ **Fendi "Baguette"**
Another iconic bag of the 21stC, this basic shape comes in a variety of fabrics, decorated or plain, for both casual and formal wear. Designed by Silvia Venturini Fendi, the "Baguette" in all its forms has become an instant collectable.

Embroidered "Baguette", 2001, Italian, signed "Fendi", **£150–250/ $225–375 (second hand)**

▲ **Prada "bowling bag"**
Miucci Prada successfully expanded her family's accessories company into clothing design, but she never lost sight of her roots. Her black nylon rucksack became a 1990s classic, and this more recent style has achieved cult status with the cognoscenti.

• Handbags that are expensive today will probably become tomorrow's most sought-after pieces. This is the case because pricier bags are usually also of higher quality and, since fewer are produced, fewer will survive.

• Dress agencies are the best source for second-hand designer bags.

▼ Anya Hindmarch

The party atmosphere at the start of the new millennium was reflected in a vogue for glitzy beads and sequins. Anya Hindmarch's exquisite take on the idea of "arm candy" advertises a brand of British sweet. Part of a series featuring various brands of sweets and crisps, this bag epitomizes the tongue-in-cheek glamour of early 21stC fashion.

Beaded bag, c.2000, English, signed "Anya Hindmarch", **£120–160/$180–240 (second hand)**

Satin and velvet bag, late 1990s, English, signed "Lulu Guinness", **£120–180/ $180–270 (second hand)**

▲ Lulu Guinness

British designer Lulu Guinness was a prime mover in the 1990s revival of 1950s-style novelty handbags. This satin bucket decorated with velvet roses is now displayed in fashion museums worldwide. Guinness's fan-shaped clutches and embroidered cottage bags are also likely to figure among tomorrow's must-have collectables. Examples of all of her bags turn up in the better dress agencies.

Japanese-style "Imro" bag, late 1990s, English, signed "Nathalie Hambro", **£300–500/$450–750 (second hand)**

▲ Nathalie Hambro

English designer Nathalie Hambro aims to "glorify humble materials" into beautiful works of art. This limited-edition bag made of steel and lead is inspired by traditional Japanese sash ornaments. Craftsmanship and design make it not only a wonderful piece to wear, but also a solid investment.

Buying & caring for vintage bags

Few dealers specialize in vintage handbags so you need to try a variety of sources in order to build a good, comprehensive collection. Start with the vintage clothing stores in your area; most carry a broad selection of handbags. Check your local telephone directory for listings. Another useful source is a large antiques centre, where stock from many different dealers is displayed under one roof. Such centres are particularly common now throughout the USA, but more are also appearing in Europe. Again, a telephone directory, antiques publications or a local tourist board will provide addresses.

Be sure to examine each unit carefully in a large antiques centre, even if you do not see a profusion of bags. Some of the best bags turn up as one-offs in general displays of antiques, and can easily be overlooked if you are moving too fast. Antiques shows, fairs and markets are also great hunting grounds, so track down the dates for your best local events and attend them

When relining antique bags, try sewing shops or specialist ribbon dealers for rosette trim such as the type shown here.

regularly. Charity, or thrift, shops occasionally produce true vintage bargains, but be aware that professional "pickers" for dealers are checking these virtually every day, so your timing must be fortuitous. Small charity boutiques in wealthy neighbourhoods, or those that benefit a specific local charity or institution such as a school, generally yield higher-quality finds than the larger, more generic charity "supermarkets". Dress agencies and exchanges can also be useful, especially for more modern "designer" bags.

The Internet is an exciting new source and a search for "vintage handbags" (or "vintage purses" as they are called in the USA) will turn up a variety of interesting sites. Internet auctions, especially "ebay", can be goldmines for great bags at great prices. The only drawbacks are that you cannot physically examine the bag before you buy, and the sheer amount of material for sale can be over-whelming. The key to "ebay" is to tailor each search to a specific type of handbag: they can be listed by era (eg 19thC bag/purse), by material (eg beaded bag/purse), by designer (eg Gucci bag/purse), or by a combination of all three (eg 1970s snakeskin Gucci bag/purse). However, no matter what it is you are after, always enter your search by ending it with the word "purse", then redo it ending with "bag", then redo it again ending with "handbag". Since terms vary from collector to collector, and between Europe and the USA, each of these endings can produce a variety of results.

Europeans tend to do better in the USA with pieces from the 1950s, 1960s and beyond, but Americans should check out the various European "ebays", where prices for 19thC and earlier bags are usually cheaper. Some auction sellers accept credit cards, and auction-oriented financial sites such as "bidpay.com" make it easy

Professional bead restoration can be very expensive and is probably only worthwhile for rarer "scenic" bags.

to pay by credit card in foreign currencies; but bear in mind that international transactions can be subject to import tax.

Many top auction companies such as Sotheby's and Christie's now run interesting websites that sometimes feature vintage fashion. While prices tend to be higher, these are good, reliable sources for the novice collector because authenticity is guaranteed.

Once your collection is underway keep it looking good by following a few simple rules. Dry-cleaning can be risky with vintage cloth bags; buy "practice" bags at a charity shop for a small amount of money and then "audition" your local dry-cleaners with these before you let them loose on any of your vintage treasures. Do not stack bags: they may look strong enough but they can easily dent or lose their shape. (Mesh bags should always be stored flat.) Store them in cloth or acid-free tissue paper. Never use bubble wrap or other plastics because these can fuse to leather, reptile or vinyl surfaces. Use string tags rather than sticky tags to label your collection. Also, lift a dealer's sticky price tag

before you buy and make sure that lacquer, finish or decorations will not be spoiled when it is removed. Replace hopelessly damaged handles with gilt chain salvaged from vintage belts or costume jewellery. Hide unremovable stains or obvious holes with decorative trimmings or appropriate patches from sewing, craft or hobby shops (see below). These can be attached with fabric glue. Beautiful antique frames are always worth buying if the price is low. Collect older fabric remnants and rehabilitate frames or restitch them to pretty bodies with damaged frames. Such projects can bring rare and prohibitively expensive styles well within reach.

However, the most important question with all vintage fashion items will always be "to wear or not to wear?" Using vintage bags is surely one of the great attractions of collecting, but this must be balanced against the fact that value is profoundly affected by condition. By all means wear and enjoy your robust, more modern finds, but some of the rarer, delicate antique bags are certainly better left for display alone.

This modern 1950s-style poodle patch covers an unsightly tear on an otherwise lovely 1950s bag.

What to read

Below is a selection of books on handbags, suitable for both new and more experienced collectors:

Dooner, Kate
Plastic Handbags
(Schiffer Publishing Ltd., Pennsylvania, 1991)

Ettinger, Roseann
Handbags
(Schiffer Publishing Ltd., Pennyslvania, 1991)

Foster, Vanda
Bags and Purses
(Batsford, London, 1982)

Haertig, Evelyn
Antique Beaded Purses
(Gallery Graphics Press, California, 2000)

Haertig, Evelyn
Antique Combs and Purses
(Gallery Graphics Press, California, 1990)

Haertig, Evelyn
More Beautiful Purses
(Gallery Graphics Press, California, 1983)

Steele, Valerie and Borelli, Laird
Handbags – A Lexicon of Style
(Rizzoli, New York, 1999)

Tolkien, Tracy
Dressing Up, Vintage
(Rizzoli, New York, 2000)

Wilcox, Claire
A Century of Style: Bags
(Apple, London, 1998)

Wilcox, Claire
Bags
(V&A Publications, London, 1999)

Where to see & buy

SPECIALIST MUSEUMS
Tassenmuseum Hendrikje
Amstelveen (near Amsterdam)
Zonnestein 1–3
1181 LR Amstelveen
Netherlands
Tel: (0031) 20 647 8681
www.tassenmuseum.nl

GENERAL MUSEUMS WITH HANDBAG COLLECTIONS
Museum of Costume
Assembly Rooms
Bennett Street
Bath BA1 2QH UK
Tel: (0044) 1225 477789
www.museumofcostume.co.uk

Victoria and Albert Museum
Cromwell Road
London SW7 2RL
UK
Tel: (0044) 20 7942 2000
www.vam.ac.uk

Smithsonian Institution
The National Mall
NW Washington DC USA
Tel: (001) 202 357 2700
www.si.edu

Metropolitan Museum of Art
1000 5th Avenue
New York
New York 10028-0198 USA

Tel: (001) 212 535 7710
www.metmuseum.org

AUCTION HOUSES
Christie's South Kensington
85 Old Brompton Road
London SW7 3LD UK
Tel: (0044) 20 7581 7611
Fax: (0044) 20 7321 3321
www.christies.com

Phillips London
101 New Bond Street
London W1Y 0AS UK
Tel: (0044) 20 7629 6602
Fax: (0044) 20 7629 8876
www.phillips-auctions.com

Sotheby's
34–35 New Bond Street
London W1A 2AA
UK
Tel: (0044) 20 7293 5000
Fax: (0044) 20 7293 5989
www.sothebys.com

Sotheby's New York
1334 York Avenue
(at 72nd Street)
New York
New York 10021
USA
Tel: (001) 212 606 7000
Fax: (001) 212 606 7016

William Doyle Galleries
175 East 87th Street
New York
New York 10128
USA
Tel: (001) 212 427 2730
Fax: (001) 212 369 0892
www.DoyleNewYork.com

UK DEALERS
Joel Rothman
Beauty and the Beast
Unit Q9-Q10
Antiquarius Antique Centre
131–141 Kings Road
Chelsea
London SW3 8DT
Tel: (0044) 20 7351 5149

Linda Bee
Gray's Mews Antiques Market
1–7 Davies Mews
London W1K 5AB
Tel: (0044) 20 7629 5921

Ruth Lane
Replay
7 Well Walk
Cheltenham
Gloucestershire GL50 3JX
England
Tel: (0044) 1242 238864

Steinberg and Tolkien
193 Kings Road
Chelsea
London SW3 5EB
Tel: (0044) 20 7376 3660

William Wain
Unit J6
Antiquarius Antique Centre
131–141 Kings Road
Chelsea
London SW3 8DT
Tel: (0044) 20 7351 4905

US DEALERS
Decades
8214 Melrose Avenue
Los Angeles
California 90046
Tel: (001) 323 655 0223

Keni Velenti
247 West 30th Street
5th Floor
New York
New York 10001
Tel: (001) 212 967 7147

Remember When
21–23 W Broad Street
Hazleton
Pennsylvania 18201
Tel: (001) 570 454 8465

Resurrection
123 East 7th Street
New York
New York 10009
Tel: (001) 212 228 0063

Vintage Haberdashery
3143 South Grand Boulevard
St Louis
Missouri 63118
Tel: (001) 314 772 1927

INTERNET AUCTIONS
www.ebay.com
www.sothebys.com

INTERNET WEBSITES
FEATURING HANDBAGS
www.chelsea-girl.com

www.enokiworld.com

www.fashiondig.com

www.jemznjewels.com

www.midnightsparkle.com

www.tias.com

www.tri-stateantiques.com/
beadedbags.html

www.vintagepurse.com

CONTEMPORARY
HANDBAG DESIGNERS
Anya Hindmarch
15–17 Pont Street
London
SW1X 9EH
Tel: (0044) 20 7838 9177

Fendi Adele Srl
Socio Unico
Sede legale
via Flaminia 968
00189 Roma
Italy
Tel: (0039) 06 330 511

Hermès GB Ltd
Knowsley House
176 Sloane Street
London SW1X 9QG
UK
Tel: (0044) 20 7259 5191

Judith Leiber
20 West 33rd Street
New York
New York 10001
USA
Tel : (001) 212 736 4244

Lulu Guinness
Third Floor
326 Kensal Road
London
W10 5BZ
UK
Tel: (0044) 20 8483 3334

Nathalie Hambro
Tel: (0044) 20 7834 1021

Paco Rabanne
6 Boulevard Du Parc
92200 Neuilly Sur Seine
Paris, France
Tel: (0033) 140 884 545

Prada
Showroom
Via Andrea Maffei 2
20135 Milano, Italy
Tel: (0039) 02 546 701

Index

Acknowledgments

Octopus Publishing Group Ltd/Steve Tanner/Steinberg & Tolkien: Front and back cover, 2, 9r, 12l, 13r, 13b, 14tl, 14tr, 14b, 15t, 15r, 15b, 16l, 17t, 17bl, 17br, 18l, 18r, 19t, 19r, 19b, 20l, 22t, 22b, 23t, 23r, 23b, 24t, 24bl, 24br, 25r, 25bl, 27t, 27b, 28r, 29t, 29bl, 29br, 30t, 30b, 31t, 31b, 32t, 32r, 32b, 33t, 33r, 33br, 34l, 34r, 35t, 35r, 35b, 36tl, 36b, 37t, 37bl, 37br, 38l, 39t, 39br, 40l, 40r, 41t, 41r, 42t, 42b, 44l, 44r, 45t, 45bl, 45br, 46l, 46r, 47bl, 47br, 48tl, 48tr, 48b, 49t, 49r, 49b, 50t, 50b, 51t, 51bl, 51br, 52l, 52r, 53t, 53r, 53b, 54l, 54r, 55bl, 55br, 59tl, 59br; Octopus Publishing Group Ltd/ Steve Tanner/Joel Rothman: 1, 5, 6t, 6b, 7, 8l, 8r, 9t, 9b, 10l, 10r, 11t, 11bl, 11br, 12r, 13tl, 16r, 20r, 21t, 21bl, 21br, 25tl, 26tl, 26c, 26br, 27r, 28l, 31r, 41b, 58bl; Octopus Publishing Group Ltd/Millers Kent/Treasures in Textiles, Cheshire: 25tr; Octopus Publishing Group Ltd/Steve Tanner/Linda Bee: 36tr, 38r, 39bl; Hermès, London: 43t, 43bl; Christie's Images: 43br; Paco Rabanne, Paris: 47t; Judith Leiber, New York: 55t; Prada, Milan: 56l; Fendi, Rome: 56r; Lulu Guinness, London: 57tl; Nathalie Hambro/ Jonathan Lovekin, London: 57r; Anya Hindmarch, London: 57b. Key: l = left, r = right, t = top, b = bottom, c = centre. The publishers would like to thank all those who contributed images and items for photography.